To I

May J...

in your life and my
prayer is for you to
grow up In God and
be a beacon light to
this dark world.
May the Lord bless you.

Shante S. K
5/16/10

No More Tears
I'm All Grown Up

Shontel D. Hightower

authorHOUSE®

AuthorHouse™
1663 Liberty Drive
Bloomington, IN 47403
www.authorhouse.com
Phone: 1-800-839-8640

First published by AuthorHouse 3/25/2010

ISBN: 978-1-4490-8534-6 (e)
ISBN: 978-1-4490-8533-9 (sc)

Library of Congress Control Number: 2010902830

Printed in the United States of America
Bloomington, Indiana

This book is printed on acid-free paper.

Introduction

This book is Shontel's second published book This book is based on a few words that got Shontel through some rough times in her life. You will also enjoy a few poems that she wrote. This book will encourage you and will allow you to be free and one thing for sure this book will minister to your very spirit. You will see that it's okay to be you and keep it real while loving the Lord at the same time. Shontel has experienced many trials and tribulations in her life. She is still fighting the good fight of faith. Many of her friends are no longer around but you can trust and be sure she still has the Lord.

Sometimes in life when we get saved we can get so caught up in church activities that we loose our selves and we stop being who we truly are. As you read this book be encouraged and believe what God has told you. Don't stand on false hope stand on the word of God and trust and believe God.

Chapter One

Suffer

Suffer-To undergo or feel pain or distress: (www.dictionary.com)

I often sit and wonder why I should or have to suffer. I pray I fast I seek God for his perfect will for my life and after I've done all of that. I suffer! I feel like I'm fighting on every hand. It's hard to wake up in the morning and keep going. So as I live for God and I love living for God let me tell you. Going back in sin is not an option after all the break up's I've endured. I suffered through the embarrassment of breaking up with someone in the church. And yet I stand for God. Its so many prayers I prayed and yet so many have gone unanswered. However I'm persuaded to keep going.

Why Lord must I suffer? Why all the pain? Why Lord? These are questions that run in my head very often. As I pondered on the word suffer I looked in my bible and came across *Philippians 1:29-For you have been given not only the privilege of trusting in Christ but also the privilege of suffering for him. (Life Application Study Bible)* After I read this I was like. Wow God for real! So I'm not giving up because I suffer I'm not turning back and living a life of no hope and drama. The devil is a liar! I have the privilege of suffering for Christ. So you may be going through right now. You may even want to give up because you think the enemy has turned the heat up. Go ahead and cry get it out. I give you that trust me I'm feeling you. But after you are done crying and you have wiped the tears from your face look in the mirror and tell yourself. You are an anointed child of God and you are not alone there are many brothers and sisters who are also suffering for the name of our Lord Jesus Christ.

So after I read the scripture over again my faith began to get strengthened and I realized I did nothing wrong. But my God has chosen me to suffer.

To God be the Glory! Stay encouraged!

Chapter two

Faith

Faith-Belief that is not based on proof: (www.dictionary.com)

o I really believe in God's promise? Is my faith where it should be? Can I continue to walk this walk even when I don't feel like it? Does God hear my prayers? You know sometimes when I'm feeling down and my attitude is not the best I just give God a hand wave. It's funny when I'm discouraged and want to give up. And God knows how I feel because I have shared it with him. Often times God will send folks my way that are stressed, tired, disgusted, and busted I think to myself God you got to be kidding me. And the person will say Shontel can you pray for me. And because my spirit says yes to God I do it. My flesh is like I'm really not in the mood for this. However I thank God for his spirit. When we read *Hebrews 11: 1-What is faith? It is the confident assurance that what we hope for is going to happen. It is the evidence of things we cannot see. (Life Application Study Bible)* I think about the person I'm praying for and I'm reminded it's not about me. So I say to myself. Now faith activate! Now faith activate in me so I can pray for this person. Faith is the confidence that I have in Christ. I have faith that God will answer that person I'm praying for. And you know what once I'm done praying I'm encouraged and then I start to believe again. I believe God will do what he says he's going to do. My faith is in Christ and not in man. My faith is not in my job or my boss. My faith is not in my money. My faith is not in my family. My faith is in Christ Jesus. So no matter how I feel or what I'm gong through I shall not be moved.

Faith! Faithfully accept in the high Priest Jesus. Keep applying faith to your life. Tell yourself. Now faith activate!

Be Blessed!

Chapter Three

Time

Each day we wake up it's a different time. Time passes by so fast. When I look back over my life of course I say if I knew then what I know now I would be this or I would be that. I've spent a lot of time on this earth being sad, depressed, broke, bitter, and mad just to name a few. I've spent time at dead end jobs not really pursuing my dreams and goals in life. Time! It just ticks away. At this point in my life I don't want to waist any more of God's precious time. I've wasted time with people who could care less about me. I've wasted time in bad relationships and it's my fault. Most of the time I knew that person was not for me. But I said to my self I'll just pass the time until something better comes along. Wasting time is what I've done for years. As I sit back and think I'm like what in the world was I thinking? I was tricked by the enemy. I felt like nothing good could happen to me. The enemy of self doubt creped in. I didn't think I could get another job or even pursue my dream as a writer. I was sitting at my work desk just wasting time. So I say all of this to say.

That was then and this is now. *Ecclesiastes 3:4-There is a time to cry and a time to laugh. There is a time to be sad and a time to dance. (The Devotional Bible-New Century Version)*

A time to cry! I did a lot of crying. Boy let me tell you I cried from age nineteen to twenty eight and now that I'm in my mid thirties I don't cry as much as I used to. (Thank God) After my mother died I was alone, bitter, and mad so I cried all the time. I cried my self to sleep so many days. And now a time to laugh. As I sat at my desk for the last three years I realized the other day I really don't laugh any more. What happened to me? I used to laugh. It was such an eye opener for me. I want to laugh again I thought to my self. I want to be me again. I want time to change. It's my time to laugh. I've had my times of sadness trust me. I was sad if my heel broke on my shoe, I was sad when my biological father wasn't ever a part of my life. For years that made me sad. Talk about depression. But I thank God that I'm no longer sad about that. Time has changed it's my time to dance.

When I was a young girl I always wanted to be a dancer. Always! After my mother died I had to focus on surviving life and now it's a new day. I want to dance. I want to dance like never before I want to Praise God with my dancing like never before.

Time! Don't let time pass away. Don't let your time on this earth be in vain. Live your life and don't allow anyone tell you not to be you. It's time for a change! It's time to make the best of your time here on earth.

Amen!

Chapter Four

Experience

Experience-Knowledge or practical wisdom gained from what one has observed, encountered, or undergone: (www.dictionary.com)

Experience! My life experience from a young women has been a bit of a ride it's been overwhelming at times. My experience with people has not been good. From a young women up until now I seem to always have drama when it comes to me and other women. I've had so called girlfriends go and talk behind my back. I've had Bishop's tell other Saints I'm too serious about God. I've had false prophesies come my way. I was once told I would be married by the time I turned thirty three. And now I'm much older than that and I'm not married yet! Experience in the church showed me that sometimes people can't take you when you are multi gifted. Did you know people despise you because you love the

Lord? I know it's hard to believe but it's true. I was once told by a man that I don't have a man because I have a bible in every room in my house. Boy that one hurt. I fell in love once and I fell hard. And I refused to bow down to the enemies plot to disrespect my body. And the young man said "well I have needs so I love you but I got to go" So he went on to be with someone who would give him what he wanted.

Experience! Even though I did not always agree with something's people said to me or the fact folks would look at me like I was crazy because I'm truly sold out and praising God. And often times I feel like no one gets me. God is still good in all of this! One day I was reading my word and I came across *Matthew 5:11-12- People will insult you and hurt you. They will lie and say all kinds of evil things about you because you follow me. But when they do, you will be happy. Rejoice and be glad because you have a great reward waiting for you in heaven. People did the same evil to the prophets who lived before you. (The Devotional Bible New Century Version)* Look at this! People will insult me people will laugh and talk about me because I love the Lord. I've been lied on and stabbed in the back by leaders, friends, and family. But you no what its okay. To God be the Glory! There were many men and women of God who suffered. For example Job, Elijah, and Joseph just to name a few and who suffered the most Jesus Christ.

My Lord had no sin he was without sin and he suffered to the death of the cross. And he rose on the third day. So I have life in God I'm free in him. At one point in my life I thought I needed to have people around me I thought I could never ever make it. After my heart got broken repeatedly I was like Lord give me a break. But experience has taught me I'm not the only one who has issues.

Experience has also taught me Bishops, preachers, and other servants of the Lord go through things and no one is perfect. Experience has taught me to rejoice and be glad life is too short to keep holding on to people, places, and things. I will also tell you life experiences will help you and I grow up.

Chapter Five

Life

What is the meaning of life? I used to ask God why did he allow me to be born. I used to ask my mother was I adopted even though I looked just like her. Funny right! I would ask her why my father didn't want me. Now that I'm older and I think about this more and I realize that God used his DNA and allowed me to enter this world. He was a part of the reason I have life. Sometimes in life you will have family members you won't get along with. I used to say to my self when I get eighteen I will never be around my mother's family. Again, I thought I was adopted. I always felt different several years after my mother died I didn't want to live. I decided to buy a gun and I thought I would visit my mother's grave and kill my self. Well one of my family members picked up on my depression or my suicidal spirit and she would not leave my house. I wanted her to leave so bad it wasn't funny. I wanted to say goodbye and do what I felt I had to do. Well to my surprise on that night in my bedroom my family members lead me to Christ. And I became a born again Christian. I was tired of life and I wanted to die so at that time in my life I thought it was crazy to live without the one person who had my back. Which was my mother? But on that day I began to live again. I said yes to Jesus. *Proverbs 8:35-Those who find me find life, and the Lord will be pleased with them. (The Devotional Bible New Century Version)* I found God so I found life. Please no that all of my problems did not disappear. Yes I still have life issues but with God on my side I have peace within. I began to understand why the Lord used my absentee fathers DNA and my beautiful mother's DNA. God needed their genes to create me. So I can do my part in this world.

Life! Now I know why I'm living God has a plan and purpose for me. Listen no matter what difficulties you have no matter what you face in life just no with Christ you can live and he will be pleased with you!

Now go out and live life. It's a gift from God!

Chapter Six

Love

**Love a profound tender, passionate affection for
another person (www.dictionary.com)**

When I was in my early twenties I feel in love I mean honey let me tell you. I was head over heels in love with this man who lived in South Jersey. I would fight for him yell at him and just act right down crazy if he did not return my calls. I went as far as to get his name tattooed on me. Yes, I know I was crazy in love. I dated this man on and off for over fifteen years of my life. I thought I could not breathe with out him I prayed that it would work out between us. When I say I would have done anything for this person trust me I would have. It's funny after the back and forth and all of the drama we had over the years. I finally had him all to my self so I thought. Wouldn't you know God would not give me any rest or peace with him? I mean I asked him to come to church with me and of course he said no. He told me the church would burn down if he walked in it. I was like I can't keep living like this I have God giving me major conviction over here and on the other hand this man doesn't want to even try and go to church with me. It was only one thing I could do and that was to leave before someone got hurt. After leaving I went through major changes in my life I realized that I made him my god. I adored him I wanted to marry him and just being in his presence meant the world to me. I loved me some him.

Love

When I left him I lost weight I was normally a size 9/10 I went down to a size 5/6. I was stressed I mean I loved him. He did not come after me and that hurt the most. I think sometimes as women we watch so many fairy tale stories we get it twisted and set our selves up for disappointment. As I sit here and reflect on some of the mistakes I made in life. One thing I realize is that I made this man my little god. And I was wrong for doing that. If I can say anything about loving another person please do not put them in the place of God. It will not work! *John 3:16- For God so loved the world he gave his only Son, so that everyone who believes in him will not perish but have eternal life. (Life Application Study Bible)* See I had to realize that there is no other love like God's love. When God sent his son on this earth that demonstrated the greatest love the best love. With loving Christ no this he is faithful. He does not cheat on us. Love hmmmmmm. What is it? It's agape.

So now that this man and I are no longer together I still love him but I love him in a different way. No we did not get married and live happily ever after. No! He did not go to church yet he still thinks the church will burn down. Trust me I'm still praying for his salvation. But moving forward I believe I know how to love now. I know how to love a man now. And I know God comes first.

Love! This word is a blessing. If you are blessed to have a mate love them with the love of Christ. Don't make them an idol. Enjoy Love!

Chapter Seven

Sacrifice

Sacrifice to surrender or give up, or permit injury or disadvantage to, For the sake of something else. (www.dictionary.com)

I feel like since I've been saved I have sacrificed so much. At one point I lost myself I was listening to folks telling me I was too sexy or I should dress like this don't forget the hat with the matching suite. Sacrifice! I once dated a minister and everyone was like oh you could be first lady. You can be a great couple. But guess what we did not really love each other. We stayed together for two years. What for? I used to ask myself this question all the time. Thank God we realized we were not in love with each other and to God be the Glory he's now married to a beautiful woman who was made just for him. Now imagine if I had listened to church folks and married the wrong man because "we looked good together" What kind of fool dog mess would that have been? That's why I'm thankful that I hear from God. I'm blessed that I did not make that kind of sacrifice and just be with someone because church folk said we look good together. Now you see if you do not study the word and seek God for yourself you will be jacked up by people. When you are single and live for the Lord there will be many temptations that will come. Sexual temptations is just one of them. Let me tell you. There is great deliverance in Christ. This is one that I struggled with. Do you want to talk about sacrifice? That man that I wrote about well that was my struggle. I prayed and I prayed and God gave me a desire to be kept. And the scripture that helped me and is still helping me is *Romans 12:1-2- So brothers and sisters, since God has shown us great mercy, I beg you to offer your lives as a living sacrifice to him. Your offering must be only for God and pleasing to him, which is the spiritual way for you to worship God. Do not change yourselves to be like the people of this world, but be changed within by a new way of thinking. Then you will be able to decide what God wants for you; you will know what is good and pleasing to him and what is perfect. (The Devotional Bible New Century Version)* So in the midst of my mess God has shown me great mercy. I thank God so much. This time in my life was so hard I used to cry myself to sleep I used to talk to one of my former coworkers and tell her I don't think I could stay strong in this area of my life. But God! So I offer my body to God as a sacrifice. I've been engaged I've had relationships. But when you let people know I'm waiting until I get married. Boy! You want to talk about demons. I was once asked. How do I know what I'm getting? The enemy will try you. But if you just pray to God trust me when you want to please God and this becomes your desire you can and will become a living sacrifice. See I refuse to change my stance just so I can have a man in my life. The Devil is a liar! I've even been called too holy. If I can share anything with you I would say. Don't change for people change for God. Don't let anyone make you feel bad because you decide to stop fornicating or lying, cheating, steeling, gambling, drugging, or whatever your addiction was. God desires you to be whole. And guess what he knows what's pleasing for you and it's not to lay up with someone who is not your spouse.

Sacrifice

At the end of the day it's worth it. But God gave the ultimate sacrifice his son Jesus who is the Christ. So don't compromise who you are for people and don't let people tell you who's for you. Let God be God!

Chapter Eight

Friendship

I learned at a young age that friends are hard to come by. All my life I never understood why it was hard for me to get along with women. I never considered myself to be a hard person to get along with. But for some reason the word jealousy always was around. When I was sixteen I thought I was ready to be an adult and lay down with someone from high school. So I went to planned parent hood and I realized having sex was not for me. To my surprise I did not have to lose my virginity to this young man a very close friend of mine slept with him for me she went behind my back and started seeing him. You want to talk about hurt and pain. I had this girl stay at my house we shared clothes we were like sisters. Since then our friendship has never been the same. I have forgiven her but that was such a devastating experience at such a young age. Later on in life I had another girlfriend of mine tell someone I was dating that I only date men with money. The funny thing was he and I were really good friends and he told me what she did. Talk about betrayal! He told me that he did not believe her and that he can see she was jealous of me. I never understood why these things happened to me. I remember when my mother was diagnosed with breast cancer. Some of her friends and family did not believe her because her hair did not fall out right away. Talk about foolishness! I remember my mother crying over her family hurting her and not being there for her during that difficult time of her life. She had friends who talked about her because she had cancer. I lived this with her so I was able to see at an early age how friends could be. But God raised up someone in her life during that time where she was able to confide in and cry to. She lives in New Jersey and after my mother died this lady this wonderful angel had my back and I'm so thankful for her.

When I got saved I was so excited I had a new life a new look and most of all I had Jesus. I had a few people that came in my life for a moment. Some women of God professed to be my spiritual mother and the painful part for me was they did not stay in my life long. They walked away. I used to wonder why. Why would someone get close to me and then drop me and never call again? Especially Spiritual Women! See with me not having a mother I was open and I think people sensed me being vulnerable and played on that at times. And I was looking for someone to fill the void I had in my heart. But after years of allowing people to get close to me I started to shut down. This was not good I used to be the life of the party I used to shut the club down. So shortly after I got saved I had one friend call me and cuss me out. When I say cussed me out I mean it. She accused me of thinking I was better than her since I was serving the Lord. And for the first time in my life I kept my mouth shut but on the inside I was burning up I wanted to flip out on her. I was so hurt. So that's when my drama with friendships started. In the four walls of the church I got hurt. One particular time I allowed someone to get close to me and this girl was my hommie. One time I shared some of my personal information with this person and she got mad at me and fussed me out because I was going through. So I prayed and the Lord led me to *Psalm 55:12-14- It was not an enemy insulting me. I could stand that. It was not someone who hated me. I could hide from him. But it is you, a person like me, my companion and good friend. We had a good friendship and walked together to God's Temple. (The Devotional Bible New Century Version)*

18

Sometimes we can deal with people insulting us but when it's people close like family and friends when it's the person you fellowship with or the person you pray with. This is when it becomes hard. If it was an enemy I could handle it. But it was those people through out my life that I let in and that hurts. But what I learned from all of these experiences is that I Shontel want and desire to be a better person I want to be a good friend to others. I had to learn that in order to forgive and heal from all of the bad friendships and relationships that I had to look at myself in the mirror. In life your friends may hurt you they may even stab you in the back. But after you get over the initial pain trust me it will make you strong. People will be people. When we allow people in and then they hurt us it can be devastating. But God is so good he has good friends for us. *Proverbs 18:24- Some friends may ruin you, but a real friend will be more loyal than a brother. (The Devotional Bible New Century Version)* So even the Lord knew some friends would try to ruin me. So this is to be expected. But a real friend will be more loyal than family. So it's all good. In this life trials and turmoil will come. But know God loves us so much he will raise up a standard.

Examine yourself and see if you are loyal friends. Believe God for the best give your best and the best will come to you. Stand strong stay on the course God has placed you on. And put your hope in God not in man.

Be Blessed,

Chapter 9

Light

Walk in the light is what I was told.

Shun darkness so God's will can unfold.

Light is who you are on this earth.

Do you see the color of salt?

It is light!

Let your light shine

The world is watching

Don't have a bad day.

Please you will never live it down.

Walk in the light

That's what I'm trying to do

Don't step into the bad side the devil is waiting for you

Run to the light

Keep going

Light, light

Jesus is God's son he is the light of the world.

Light

Psalm 27:1-The Lord is my light and the one who saves me. I fear no one. The LORD protects my life; I am afraid of no one. (The Devotional Bible New Century Version) Psalm 18:28-LORD, you give light to my lamp. My God brightens the darkness around me. (The Devotional Bible New Century Version) So God let the light of your son shine in and on me. In all the dark places in my life Father brighten it up. You are King! You are everything you are my light.

Chapter Ten

Safety

Can I trust you?

Are you someone I can share my thoughts with?

Can I be myself in your presence?

Will you judge me because I like to have fun?

Are you safe?

Felling safe hasn't been an option for me in years.

When people see your weaknesses it seems to turn them off.

Private conversations taking my mask off in front of you allowing you in.

Safe!

I thought you were safe.

But you turned away from me and made fun.

Are you safe?

Mommy is gone now no longer do I feel safe.

My world has turned upside down no one to trust.

You think I have a chip on my shoulder.

I guess I do!

I don't feel safe anymore.

Please don't judge me.

Please no one disrespect me.

I feel like I am going to explode.

Don't you see I have to make it in this life?

I'm looking for safety please don't hate on me.

I'm not trying to out shine you but I'm running for my life.

I see a safe house up ahead

Oh I'm running to Jesus!

I'm now safe.

Chapter Eleven

Engagement

Sometimes in life we get to a point when we want to get married. We want to share our life with someone. At one time in my life I think I prayed for a husband for five years. Coming to Christ out of a life of hip hop, drugs, alcohol, and Ballers. It wasn't easy being by my self. Before I got saved I used to smoke so much weed it was not funny I started smoking at the age of fifteen and stopped when I was twenty seven. I know that's a long time. Giving up some of my music like Biggie and Mary J was difficult I had allowed these people to become an idol in my life. Moving on I wanted to be married. I thought when I got saved and walked down the aisle all of my problems would disappear and then I thought I would get the perfect man who loves God would come my way and we would get married serve God and live happily every after. Not! This is one of my testimonies. I have been prophesied to so many times that your husband is coming. That prophesy came two years in a row. After a while its like come on Jesus I'm trying here I really want to be kept. I'm fasting and praying and all of this and I was getting nothing but counterfeit men. You want to talk about being discouraged.

One day I ran into an old friend from a long time ago and I was saved and he was saved. Sounds good to me so we started dating one another so a few months after we started dating he asked me to marry him and I said yes I will marry you boy. But deep down in my heart I was not happy with him. I have nothing against this person but he was not my covering he was not able to lead me spiritually. He purchased me a very beautiful two karate diamond ring I absolutely adored the ring. The bad part about the ring is he kept saying to me that he bought me the ring. Can you imagine the person you said yes to the person you are going to spend the rest of your life with complaining about buying you a ring? Talk about being turned off. He kept saying I spent all this money on that ring. The bottom line is he did not want to wait to go to bed with me so he thought by buying me the ring that would have been the green light to fornicate. Wrong! I kept thinking to myself how could I marry someone that put a ring on it and then want me to bow down and go to bed with him. Now I really cared for this person but I did not love him to the point where I wanted to throw away my anointing from God on him. So I know in my heart I was not for him and he was not for me. After praying and thinking about my situation I decided to give him back the ring and he grabbed it so fast I wanted to bust out laughing. I guess he felt the same way.

It is so important for you and me to marry the right person. If I had married this man I would have died. He was not my covering he was not my perfect fit. Sometimes God will have you marry someone out of obedience to him. For example when Mary became pregnant by the Holy Spirit she had to tell Joseph and after telling him he was not going to marry her. However in *Matthew 1:20-21-While Joseph thought about these things, an angel of the Lord came to him in a dream. The angel said, "Joseph descendant of David, don't be afraid to take Mary as your wife, because the baby in her is from the Holy Spirit. She will give birth to a son, and you will name him Jesus, "because he will save his people from their sins." (The Devotional Bible-New Century Version)* See Joseph had doubt however an angel came and spoke to him and he obeyed. That's why it's important to pray and listen to God. Please do not marry the wrong person. You need someone in your life to support you, love you, and respect you. See I had a lot of doubt but I knew in my heart it was not of God. And believe it or not I was tired of waiting I had no right to be this way but I was tired. But God had mercy on me and did not allow me to be in a marriage with someone who was not for me. It matters who you are connected to.

Engagement is important but marriage that's a covenant relationship before God. Whatever decision you make please be sure you are lead by the Holy Spirit. Don't accept someone's proposal if you know deep in your heart that person is not for you. Remember we have to be mindful of other people's feelings!

Be Blessed,

Chapter Twelve

Betrayal

**Betrayal –to disappoint the hopes or expectations
of; be disloyal to: (www.dictionary.com)**

The first time I ever felt betrayed was back in high school. How do you know if you've been betrayed? I felt betrayed by my mother's family. When she died I had no one. It's funny my mom's funeral was jammed packed with family and friends. The balcony of the church was even packed. And after the casket went down in the ground I realized that's it. Shon you are on your own. So a few weeks went by and I did not want to stay at one of my family member's house because my mother had died in their house. So my family member said to me "you have to be in my house by midnight because I have a teenage daughter to raise and I have to set an example for her." Little did this person know I was coming in late was because my mother had died in that house. So I was so hurt by this but this is when I started to grow up. So two weeks later I moved out. I was bitter and angry how could this person tell me to come and stay in a house where my mother my best friend died and took her last breath. This was also the family member who said "I will never make it in life because I was spoiled by my mother" Looking back her betrayal was the best thing for me. Of course it hurt until no end and I was all alone and I suffered. But God had my back all the way. I couldn't understand why God would first take my mother and then allow me to be apart of a family that was jacked up all around. My answer for this is I still don't get it. (Smile)

Why does God allow us to be betrayed? Why do hurtful things happen? Why do we have to suffer? I struggled for years wondering if I even mattered to God.

The Ultimate Betrayal

Mathew 26:48-50-Judas had planned to give them a signal saying "the man I kiss is Jesus. Arrest him." At once Judas went to Jesus and said, "Greetings, teacher!' and kissed him. Jesus answered, "Friend, do what you come to do." *Then the people came and grabbed Jesus and arrested him. (The Devotional Bible New Century Version)* What's deep about this? Jesus knew he was going to be betrayed he saw it coming. When Judas bought the people with him Jesus greeted him as a friend he said friend do what you have to do. This ministered to me. Guess what? I feel like this friend do what you have to do. Family do what you have to do. Because at the end of the day you are doing what you want to do. People will sell you out for money, people will sell you out for a man, and people will sell you out just because. What I liked about this Jesus remained calm and basically said do you. Now that's gangsta! At the end of the day I had to realize that I can't stop people from being who they are. But I know one thing for sure you will reap what you sew!

Matthew 27:3-5- Judas, the one who had given Jesus to his enemies, saw that they had decided to kill Jesus. Then he was very sorry for what he had done. So he took the thirty silver coins back to the priest and leaders, saying, "I sinned; I handed over to you an innocent man." The leaders answered. "What is that to us? That's your problem, not ours." So Judas threw the money into the Temple. Then he went off and hanged himself. (The Devotional Bible New Century Version) Judas became sorry for what he did guilt over came him. So he wanted to make it right. And the priests did not care they had Jesus. So the next step for Judas was suicide.

Even though I did not understand my family when my mother passed away. I was nineteen and hurt and to have my own family turn their back on me at the lowest point in my life was very hurtful. But I can't nail them to the cross. That's between them and God. But after reading this I know one thing for sure if you do someone dirty you will not have rest or peace.

Judas could not live with him self. So he ended his life. The betrayal that Judas demonstrated was for our God because Jesus had to go to the death of the cross and rise. So we could have life. Sometimes being betrayed is good for us. Look at Jesus he has all power. And after my family not being there for me I'm still here. And no it's not a happy ending my family and I are not close and it has been a strained relationship. But I'm grateful because God did not allow me to fail. To God be the Glory!

Betrayal

I thought you had my back

I thought you loved me

The whole time you were holding out on me

I confided in you from the start

Thinking we were friends

Betrayal was in your heart

You didn't want me to prosper

How could I get ahead of you?

In life!

Oh no I will not allow that to happen

That's what you said

So I will sabotage your destiny

That was your plot

But in the end

It was self destruction on your own life

You didn't want me to be his wife

Mind games you played betraying me girl

You had it bad

In the end God has the final word

Look at Judas he killed his self

His betrayal was not worth it

The kiss of death is what you gave me

Look at you now

Acting like you love me

But I see you for who you are

Betrayal!

Chapter Thirteen

Apology

*Definition for apology-A written or spoken expression of
one's regret, remorse, or sorrow for having insulted, failed,
injured, or wronged another. (www.dictionary.com)*

This is my written apology to someone I loved a long time ago. If I could turn back the hand of time and just sit and talk to you I would. Looking back over the years we were Bonnie and Clyde to the end. A ghetto love is what we had. Tattoo of your name on my back a portrait of me on your leg a three year bid I stuck by your side. You really know me. Soul mates from the start eighteen years ago our first date. I was feeling you. We ran after each other playing games back and forth acting like we did not care for each other. I was your ride or die chick till death due us part is what we had. I was your wife separation was not in the equation.

Baby what happened. Running the streets is what we both did. I loved your kids like they were my own. What ever I had to do just to have you. I didn't feel burdened being with you. I had a vision of us sitting under a tree on a swing forty years later. I used to have fits of rage because I did not get my way with you. I'm an only child and I had so many issues you just did not understand. I miss you to death and this is the truth. Every chapter of my life you were there. This love thing I don't understand. I tried to leave so many times but I kept running back to you. I understand you don't like to talk that much just sitting in your presence was good enough for me. Where did I go wrong? I held you down. You have my heart and I tried to let you go. I ran to the church just to help me cope with this love I had for you. I confided in so called friends that told me to leave you. I was starting a new life with God and having you was hard. At the time I did not know how to love God and you at the same time.

Apology

You came home one day and I snapped not allowing you to grow. I walked out on you and the kids this was a mistake. Folks telling me to run for my life and don't look back. I ran away from home and didn't look back. I didn't handle the situation like a real woman. And I apologize. This is my letter to you. I tried to have other relationships but none of them could compare to you. I became a people pleaser and tried not to love you. So now you have another life and I'm not in it. I stand at the door looking in. Sometimes I wish we could be together this is a thought in my head. However reality sets in and I realize I walked out on you. With no explanation I betrayed you because I allowed church folks to have control over me. The lesson I learned life does go on. Oh did I tell you I'm so very proud of you. You kept it moving. A successful business man you have become. So I often sit and reminisce about our time we had. Bonnie and Clyde to the end. You were my perfect fit from the start no other man has ever had my heart the way you did. I know I have the Lord but life is meaningless without a companion.

Ecclesiastes 4:9-12-Two people are better than one, because they get more done by working together. If one falls down, the other can help him up. But it is bad for the person who is alone and falls, because no one is there to help. If two lie down together, they will be warm, but a person all alone will not be warm. An enemy might defeat one person, but two people together can defend themselves. A rope that is woven of three strings is hard to break (The Devotional Bible New Century Version) I often read this passage and wondered why it's so hard to move on in my heart. God knows I prayed and prayed but on today I don't care what the church people think I'm being true to the game. The love I have for you never left you still are in my heart I've compared other men to you which was not fare. But I had to apologize to you. If I ever hurt you from my actions I didn't know how to be saved. So as I began to have a personal relationship with God I see my mistakes. I love the Lord with all of my heart and as I seek him more and more I realized the love I had for you I never let it go. So this apology is for you. Maybe this chapter is closure for me or maybe it's a new beginning but whatever it is it is truly well with my soul. I will always have memories of you.

So I'm being real with my self and others. To all of the men that came in and out of my life if I ever hurt you I apologize to you from my heart. I was finding my self in God. One of the points I want to share with those of you who are reading this book is be real with yourself and God. The Lord loves you and the best thing you can do is be obedient to God in all you say and do. Please take it from me don't let people in church tell you how to be or how to act or dress. And what God has for you is for you. Learn from my mistakes trust God and not people God is real and I believe he will make it plain.

Psalm 37:4-Take delight in the Lord and he will give you your heart's desire. (Life Application Study Bible) I have taken delight in the Lord and I know he will give me the desires of my heart, and now I know God has my best interest at hand. Trust God and not people this is the first time I've been open and real about the love of my life. And I feel good I tried to surpress my feelings but at the end of the day it is what it is. Now I can move on.

Real Love

Real love is what we had

I was a ride or die from the start

No one better raise a tongue against you

I would flip out on them

I protected my love I had for you

You were my boo

I tried to leave you alone so many times

So I had to keep it real with God and stop lying to myself

Real love is hard to come by

But at least I can say I experienced it at least one time

So as I sit and type this poem

No more wasting time on the past

And what I did

I apologize for walking out

See I made a mistake and made you my little god

And for that I was wrong

So I went to God and repented

Now I know I can love God and have a place for you in my heart

I had to heal and now I can be real

You were the one I held close to my heart

Are you feeling me?

Hey!

Thank you for loving me for me

Real love

Chapter Fourteen

Temptation

I t's so much temptation surrounding me all these men trying to put a hold on me. Running for my life I'm trying to win this race that's before me

Every time I meet a man of God he tries to get in my bed

You making me look at you sideways

Deep down inside I know you are not the one

How can you live a double life?

When you trying to sleep with me

Now I realize no one is perfect

I know this to be a fact

But all of ya'll the same

Temptation said I'm too Holy

She really loving the Lord

High standards yes I raised the bar

Why can't you come up?

Why must I come down there just to be with you?

Temptation please get behind me

It's a shame that I see you for who you are

Go and run your game on someone else

It's old and tired

I see you and so does God

At the end of this life we all will have to give an account for our selves

Temptation I don't like you

Will the real men of God please stand up?

Stop allowing the temptress get to you

Matthew 6:13-Lead us not into temptation but deliver us from evil (King James Version)

Don't you read your word?

If you can't be kept

That's fine with me

Just don't try to take me with you

What you see is what you get?

Temptation

Please stop knocking at my door

Fighting the thought of sexual sin that's within

Then here you come wanting me to react

Luring spirits you carry

Knowing I'm trying to stay delivered from that money demon

Back up off of me

Don't you see I'm running?

Temptation keep chasing me down

Men keep telling me they can wait

But the truth is after the first date

Now you think I will be your mate

Temptation you got to be kidding me

No more drama

No I don't want to be your baby mamma.

I know my worth God told me Psalm 139:14-I praise you because you made me in an amazing and wonderful way. What you have done is wonderful. I know this very well. (The Devotional Bible New Century Version)

So temptation don't you see

God made me wonderfully made

God thinks high of me I know temptation will come

But I'm confronting ya

I'm down for the Lord

Can't turn back now

I plead the blood over my situation

Temptation

I no longer love you

No more playing with your conversation

The lust of you I don't want any more

So my final word for temptation

Leave me alone

Go play with someone else

It's over

I got so much temptation surrounding me all these men trying to put a hold on me. Acting like they love me.

Just to get me to commit fornication they don't want to put a ring on it.

Then they say oh you trying me.

Come on let's go to Tiffany's two karats later and now you want me to sin.

Boy are you crazy!

Get to know me is what I say.

But no you are trying to lay all in my bed.

Beating me in the head with your boring conversation

No substance to what you are saying.

I reminisce of the love I once had.

I had a bad boy for life.

But I had it bad.

Loving him deep in my soul.

I can't love him I want a crown of gold.

A saved man is what I wanted I went from one extreme to another.

You are a fraud.

That's who you are

Playing church just to get in the pants

Why God didn't you let me keep my bad boy?

At least I knew his love for me was real.

To all the counterfeit church men

Be who you are going to be.

Because you are confusing me.

You will catch more bees with honey.

God really sees you for who you are.

God created man in his own image.

Come on man of God win that race that's before you.

Stop your foolishness!

Chapter Fifteen

Real Words

When I was five my cousin tried to molest me. I remember like it was yesterday. I also remember my mother and her sisters were going to kill him. But my grand pop said "he would handle it". And guess what he did not. I don't know if he tried to keep the peace or what. But you know if a Pedi file is not taken care of or dealt with he will strike again. Thank God he healed me from this. My prayer is for men, women, boys, and girls who have been molested or rapped is for God to heal them. When I was twelve my girlfriends uncle tried to rape me he was eighteen. I just don't get it. Why? I often sit and wonder why some people would choose to abuse others and hurt others. Its so many hard things that I had to endure in my life but when grown folks decide to mistreat and abuse children it makes me sick to my stomach. As I've gotten older I realize I had to forgive those people who hurt me I have to walk in this. *Mathew 6:12-Forgive us for our sins, just as we have forgiven those who sinned against us. (The Devotional Bible New Century Version)* When

I pray to God and ask for forgiveness I have to pray for those who sinned against me and truly forgive them. Who am I not to forgive someone? It's Christ who died on the cross not me. So allow your self to forgive just as Christ forgave us.

Forgiveness

I pray to forgive you

I seek God to forgive you

Do you no how much you hurt me?

Let it Go

Let it go

Let it go and flow with that

Let it go and ride with that

Let it go and let God be God

Let it go and look to the sky

Let it go and just be you

Let it go and spread your wings

Let it go and do the darn thing

Let it go and praise the Lord

Let it go and do your dance

Let it go and stop living in the past

Let it go

Love

Love, Love, Love

I'm feeling you

But!

You don't want me loving you back

So many rules I can't take it

I just want to be real with you

But I feel like I have to put on a mask and pretend I don't like you

But deep in side I really do want you.

Love

Come my way

Love

Please don't stray

Love

Can't you see I need you love?

Love, love

If I would sing a song I would be so real with you

Mind blowing love would make me

But I realize love don't love me

If I could sing this would be my melody

Love, love

Real love is what I'm searching for

The one who I can adore

Be my self with

Where we can put the games on the shelf and be real adults

That's how I see love

Would love to get excited when I see your name on the caller ID

Feeling butterflies all inside of me

What did you say love?

I want to adore you

Take long walks talking until dark

I see the vision that's before me

When will it become reality?

Love,

Do you even like me?

Embrace

Embrace the new don't be afraid

The worst has already happened

Life is a gift and we have to embrace it

See it for what it is

The truth is right in your face

Embrace it

Embrace people

Embrace change

Embrace the fact that you are still alive

It's a new day

Embrace it!

I'm doing me

The Power of God lives in me

It's no denying

That's why I'm trying to win this race before me

Stop sitting there hating

It's the God in me

That keeps me pressing towards heaven

So why you looking at me

Realize I'm free

In God that is

So be all that you can be for Christ you see

Because I'm doing me

The Power of God lives in me

So I'm pressing towards the mark

Straight from the start

It's the Power of God that lives in me

So stop hating because I'm free

I'll say it again

I'm doing me!

This poem is dedicated to a women by the name of Jackie whom I never had the opportunity to met she was a friend of one of my co-workers (Tracy a.k.a Miss H) and she told me how she was suffering from the disease called Cancer. A few days after the Lord gave me the words to write to her she passed away. She never had a chance to hear or read this poem. I'm still praying for her family and friends. Rest in Peace!

Jackie

This poem that I write is just for you

Please know that I'm praying for you

I know you are not ready to leave your family behind

But stand on the word of God

He will never leave you nor forsake you.

To be absent from the body is to be present with the Lord.

God has seen all of the love you gave to others and he knows you are adored

You are a blessing

So rest in God he has your back

You're well thought of Jackie please know that

This poem that I write is just for you

You don't know me but I'm praying for you

Please don't be afraid there is no fear in God

Again I say rest in Jesus

He's waiting on the other side

Of heaven that is

Jackie you are an angel! And God sees the light in you.

So again I say! Rest in God he loves you my dear

Prayer

Dear Heavenly Father in the name of Jesus

This prayer is to you

I ask that you keep me today

Please guide and protect me all the way

Keep my thoughts on you

Please forgive me of my sins in the name of Jesus

Father please keep the hand of the adversary away on today.

Open the doors that you want me to walk in and close every door that is not of you

In Jesus name

Father bless those who are less fortunate than me in the name of Jesus

Bless my brothers and sisters on lock down in the name of Jesus

Father I ask that you bless our young people don't allow them to stray in the name of Jesus

Father I love you and I submit my will and desires to you on today

Order my steps on today in the name of Jesus

Bless those who do not know you on today

And father touch this world the way that you know how and Father what ever

I failed to pray fail not to grant on my behalf

In Jesus name I pray

Amen!

No More Tears/I'm all grown up

No more tears

I'm all grown up now

Tired of feeling blue

It's time to live now

I grew up kind of fast

I had so much drama in my past

I had a lot of friends

They are no longer around

Love lost I used to be down

I'm all grown up

Can't run home to momma

She went home to be with the Lord

Daddy left a long time ago

You see I had a reason to be sad

Walking in darkness for so many years

I thought that's how life was supposed to be

So many tears fell from my eyes

Didn't think God even realized that I was here on earth

I used to think why did God allow my momma to give birth to me

I'm all grown up

Searching for real love I thought it would have come in the form of a man

Tired of doing things on my own

I'm all grown up

Through the up's and the down's

I'm still here

I never thought God had a plan

No more tears

Tired of crying over the things of the past

It's a new day and I want to enjoy it

Rest in peace Mother

I'll see you again

Daddy I forgive you for not being my Dad

I'm no longer holding you to the things of the past.

No more tears

To my cousin who sexually abused me

I forgive you

I'm all grown up

To my family

I love you

By you not having my back it helped me to grow up fast

I'm tired of holding on to my past

It's not your fault

Life it what it is

Grandmother keeps the faith

You are my sister in Christ

I love you to life

Moving forward in the things of God

No more crying over the past

I release my self into the new

I'm tired of you devil trying to make me feel blue

I'm free in Jesus can't you see

To all my real hommies you no who you are

No more crying we got to keep it moving

God has plans

No more Tears/*what's done is done*

I'm all grown up/*No more looking back*

Release Me

This is the year of restoration

This is the time of God's total release

How do I know?

I can feel it in my spirit

Release me into my destiny

Release me into my purpose

Release me from my debt

Release me to the nations

I feel the power of God all in me

He's telling me to go and possess the land

No more excuses

No more fears

I'm released to lend and not borrow

I'm released to be a blessing to others

I'm released from my past failures

This is a new day in God.

The season has changed.

And God has released you and me to go out into the land and do his will!

Release

Words from the Author

When I got saved I hid my self in the church from the world and got involved in every ministry that I could. After rededicating my life to Christ I decided to get baptized again the first time I got baptized I was twelve years old and I was so happy. The second time was February 2002 All Star Weekend in Philadelphia, PA. If any one knows me from my past knows how I had love for my Balla's. The Sunday I got baptized one of my friends I used to party with called me and had a free ticket for me to go to the game. I turned it down instead I made a decision to go all the way with God. So that Sunday at Sharon Baptist Church in Philadelphia, PA I went down in the water. I realized at that point I was really sold out for Christ! I loved the Lord so much I was open and I believed that others were sold out. But over the years I've discovered that many people I allowed in my life did not mean me any good. Without my mother in my life I was open. I was open to hurt open for love and open to many disappointments I was looking for a real friend and could not find it. So eight years later I decided to be real with myself. To love my self again and realize that being saved does not mean dying literally just walking around existing because I was sad I was depressed even with Christ. I allowed people to hurt me. But today is a new day. This book is inspired by the Holy Spirit. God has allowed me to be free in him. People will come and go and that's fine with me. But what really matters is my relationship with Christ. So I pray you enjoy this book I've decided to share a few words that has helped me grow and helped me to become free in Christ. I've also added a few poems to this book for you to enjoy. My prayer is that you will really be blessed and I pray that some of the chapters really minister to you.

God Bless,

Shontel

Acknowledgments

I would like to thank my Lord a Savior Jesus Christ for once again pouring into me. I would like to thank those who have gone home to be with the Lord. Esselyn D. Hightower-Murray (Mommy I will never forget you) James Hightower Jr. (Grand pop I miss you so much) Debbie Brown (I miss having tea with you) Craig Hannah (My true friend I really miss you)

I also would like to thank my god-mother Minister Sharon Bennett I know you are praying for me. Miss Sylvia Wyche-Fitzgerald (Miss Peachy I thank God for you) V. Imani Bennett (PA) I can't wait to read your book, Marvella D. Withers-Lopez I'm glad we have gotten closer, Tahira Morris thank you for pushing me and always asking how's the book coming along. Tawanna Donaldson thank you for supporting me I appreciate you. Latanya Anderson I value our personal conversations. Tracy Pryor (sister) I'm so glad you are in my life I love you and you are still my she-ro thanks for doing a great job on my hair. Robin D. Hughes girl what can I say I thank you for being there when I needed you the most. Keep running this race for God. Shani Bayette I appreciate all of your support. Lexlie Jefferson I want to thank you for all of the love and support you gave me when my mother passed away you helped me to become a responsible woman. I would also like to thank my church family Freedom Christian Bible Fellowship Church in Philadelphia, PA. Thank you all for supporting my first book, I appreciate it. Minister Jackie Odrick thank you for supporting the vision God has given me. To my co-workers thank you for supporting me in my endeavors. Michael L. Murray I'm glad you are my dad I love you. To the Cheeks family thank you for coming back in my life you guys have been a blessing to me this past year. Dorothy H. Smith (grandmother keep writing your tracts you are such a blessing to the body of Christ) Minister Sondra Cartwright (State-Mom) what can I say I love you, I love you, and I love you. Nia Lott thank you for doing such a great job with my make-up. Gregory Evans thank you for coming into my life at the right time. To all of my hurting people out there please know that I'm praying for you. To my brothers and sisters on lock down I'm praying for you too.

Be Blessed,

Hair Stylist

Tracy Pryor/Calvin's Upscale Salon

Tracypryor@hotmail.com

Make up Artist

Nia Lott/Purpose by Design Inc.

NLott@purposebyDesigninc.com

Photographer

Sondra Cartwright/Through His Eyes

Sgimages@aol.com

About the Author

*A*fter years of turmoil and drama, Shontel felt a strong desire for change. She knew that there had to be more to life than what she was experiencing. Beaming with joy, Shontel proclaims that the best day of her life was when she accepted the Lord Jesus Christ into her heart as her personal savior. The lasting lesson she learned from the tough times was that God is in control no matter what she has been through or will go through in life. If she truly submitted her life to Christ she can experience life again and have joyous times continually.

As an author, performance poet, dancer, songwriter, rapper, screenwriter, entrepreneur, creative genius, and an energetic and blazing speaker, Shontel is dedicated to helping others overcome their struggle.

Breinigsville, PA USA
11 May 2010
237811BV00001B/6/P